MW00878971

40 Days to Freedom

A Lenten Practice for the Modern Mind

Written by Michelle Wadleigh
Compiled and Edited by Alice Reid

Copyright © 2011 by Michelle Wadleigh and Alice Reid.

Library of Congress Control Number:		2011900585
ISBN:	Hardcover	978-1-4568-3030-4
	Softcover	978-1-4568-3029-8
	Ebook	978-1-4568-3031-1

All rights reserved. No part of this book may be reproduced or transmitted in any form or by any means, electronic or mechanical, including photocopying, recording, or by any information storage and retrieval system, without permission in writing from the copyright owner.

This book was printed in the United States of America.

To order additional copies of this book, contact:
Xlibris Corporation
1-888-795-4274
www.Xlibris.com
Orders@Xlibris.com
89389

To Ilona,
Promise yourself +
no suffering - ever.
Love,
Michelle

This book is dedicated to the individual who knows that they are a Divine Emanation of Spirit but somewhere along the line, lost their way in the complexity of life. Here is your lifeline.

The world has learned all it should
through suffering. We do not say that
we have learned all we ever shall
through suffering; we affirm that we
should not have to suffer in
order to evolve.

—Ernest Holmes

Acknowledgments

I am so blessed for the influences, love, and support that I have received throughout my lifetime. And I would like to begin with thanking the single most important influence of my life who no longer walks this earth, Reverend Dr. Rita Sperling Rogers—the founder of the Planned Happiness Institute, a place where hearts were healed and minds were transformed. Thank you to my Science of Mind teacher, Reverend Frankie Timmers, and the influences of so many other teachers such as the Reverend Dr. Michael Beckwith.

Thank you to my mother, Mary Agnes Flynn, and my father, Clifford Harvey Wadleigh, my three sons: Michael Sarnowski and Keith Sarnowski, and Seth Wadleigh, and a special thank you to my nephew, John Kweselait. Also my neighbor and friend Gesa Nichols, my friends Joe Schneider and Marcy Schneider, Bill Sarnowski and Marilynn Sarnowski, and to my congregation who have supported my growth and believed in me without fail.

I love and honor you all.
Michelle Wadleigh

I wish to acknowledge my mother, Patricia Phillips, who opened almost every gate I have passed through on my spiritual journey by walking through them first. It is through her enthusiasm for personal and spiritual growth that I first found my hunger for Spirit; and to my husband, James Reid, who demonstrates to me each day how to love unconditionally. It is a gift to be loved so completely. And to my children, Jonathan Reid and Emma Matthews, and my grandchildren, Elijah, Faith, and Isaac, who remind me constantly what is really important in life.

I am grateful to my prayer partners and to my students who know who they are. They have each in their own way been lovely company along this journey of mine. To Michelle, for her openhearted Jersey girl self—we are indeed kindred spirits. And finally, I acknowledge my teacher, the late

Reverend Dr. Jeffrey Proctor. I am grateful for his brilliance, his love, and of course, his patience as he held me in my truth despite my reluctance to accept my own worthiness. His influence has forever changed me for the better; I can only pray that one day I will pay his generosity forward.

Warmly,
Alice Reid

Introduction
You Were Born Perfect!

This statement should not shock you; this should be a statement simply affirming what you already know. But alas, most of us don't arrive at adulthood knowing this truth about ourselves or should I say remembering this truth. Some of us do not even complete adolescence remembering our perfection; in other words, we've already forgotten by our teen years.

There seems to be some Divine design that causes us to slowly forget our perfection as we grow up. And then the game of life begins and becomes one of attempting to remember and reconnect to our Divinity. We spend thousands of hours and loads of money taking classes, workshops, and seminars, reading self-help books, going to therapy, and sometimes surrendering to a program of medication, all because we forget. We forget our earliest knowing that we were born perfect, divine, strong, and beautiful. If we remembered our perfection none of this would be necessary.

There is, however, a place in you that exists that was never hurt, harmed, or injured in any way. Yes, at the core of your being is the full, perfect you. It is the very thing that carries you, calling to you to remember. It is probably the reason that you picked up this book. Your intuition resides in this protected place that has remained unharmed through your entire life. It is time for you to remember; it is time for you to come home to your truth that this place exists within and this is eternal.

This workbook has been designed to support *remembering* who you are. This book has been created with the full knowledge that if you could remember who you are in your fullness, be completely in touch with your power, loving and accepting yourself exactly as you are in this *moment*, there would be no need for any of these exercises.

The discontent that you might be experiencing in your life has been created over years of lazy, unproductive, habitual thinking where you carry anger, resentment, and judgments about yourself and others that perpetuate your state of discontent and aid in your losing touch with your innate, divinely ordained *Godspark*.

This workbook does not attempt to "create" anything in you that does not already exist. You were born perfect! These tools are designed to support you in moving beyond the habits, belief systems, and thought patterns that have distracted you from the experience of your inherent magnificence, fully expressed as only you can express it. This journal is an invitation to take on some daily thinking and behavior habits that will support your return to *you* and the *Godspark* within you.

We invite you to jump in courageously and take these suggestions seriously. Carry this journal with you and pay attention to what comes up for you as you do these exercises. Give yourself the gift of setting aside a few moments each day to weed out any thoughts or beliefs that no longer serve you so that you can make room for a bigger, more potent truth to emerge. 40 days is a small investment to make to retrieve yourself and remember who you came here to be.

Namasté, Michelle Wadleigh and Alice Reid

40-Day Lenten Practice

We are living in a very interesting time, a time of extremes. One can easily find evidence today for the spiritual advancement of humankind and simultaneously see evidence of where humankind has not progressed at all. Everywhere we look there are groups of people sprouting up who are choosing to take a stand for something wonderful, something spiritual, or at a subtle level, something peaceful. These groups grow silently as a subculture, and as we begin to look for them, we will begin to see them everywhere. Yet pick up the newspaper or turn on the television to watch the international news and we see evidence of our collective, yet unconscious, resistance to the global good. Evidence that appears as war, genocide, and suicide car bombings continue to serve as a reminder of the work that is left for us to do to transform our world.

Why is it our job to transform the world? It is ours to do if we consider ourselves awake; once we make this decision, we must consider ourselves responsible. It is through our awareness and our compassionate caring that the world will continue to transform into a loving, compassionate, and life-giving place to live. Does this mean, however, we are required to go out and "save" the world or campaign on a street corner? No; our only job is to heal and reveal our wholeness to the best of our ability in each and every moment. There is no private good, and as we individually raise our level of consciousness, all of who we are will express itself more wholly. And through this wholeness, our innate good will be revealed.

The *40 Days to Freedom Practice* can be used in a few different ways. It can be used during the Christian time of Lent as a modernized and more empowering Lenten practice, or it can be used simply as a mind fast any time of the year. It can be used individually, with a group, or along with a prayer partnership.

This is a powerful, mindful, and effective practice that calls us to a higher order. This Lenten Practice is not about giving up what we love or physically fasting from food. During this practice, you can eat when and what you like. Although if you choose to fast, a healthy physical fast is always good for the spirit; we'll talk more about fasting later. This Lenten Practice is about learning how to grab and hold your own attention and redirect it to creating and recreating healthier, more empowering thinking habits. Our thoughts precede our actions and so to live a healthier, happier, and more expressed life, it is imperative that we improve upon our conditioned mental status. In other words, we are here to rise above our conditioning, or as Don Miguel Ruiz likes to say, we can rise above our "domestication."

The 40-Day Lenten Practice is about fasting from negative, limiting, self-denigrating thoughts. You can do as much or as little as you like, but the more committed you are to this practice, the more you will accomplish. Not only are you invited to fast from negative thinking habits and, most specifically, from all judgments, you will be asked to refrain from gossiping, blaming, complaining, and, most importantly, from self-loathing for 40 days.

A Note to All Our Religious Traditionalist Friends

This 40-Day Lenten Practice is meant to be used any time of the year, although, for many, you will probably want to use this during the time of Lent. The 40-day practice can be used between Ash Wednesday and Easter as a way to renew a spiritual practice that you *wanted to love* but never did. If you fall into the category of one who used to practice Lent and it left you a little empty, you can use this 40-day practice to have a powerful experience during this sacred time of year.

Lent, as it was taught, has some elements within it that we would like to address here to support you in this journey.

Repentance

Oh yes, that good old idea of earning your place in heaven through suffering and sacrifice is not part of this practice. In this 40-day Lenten Practice, if you feel compelled to *repent*, consider forgiving yourself first. Forgive yourself for all past and present indiscretions so that you may be present to this process. If you must, acknowledge the behavior or decisions that you made that do not make up your proudest moments, write them down on a piece of paper, forgive yourself, and then *burn* the paper. Release your guilt, sin, blame, and shame. This would be an appropriate time to point out that in this text *sin* means to make a mistake or to miss the mark rather than an action or behavior that only God can release you from.

How can we say this so easily? Because love, acceptance, compassion, and forgiveness cannot occupy the same space as guilt, sin, blame, and shame. If your desire is for spiritual liberation or to walk in the light and love of God, then you must be available, and you cannot be available if you are preoccupied with guilt.

Each and every day you make better decisions, and as you go through these 40 days and tap into a new aspect of yourself as Spirit, your decisions will be reflected in this new, available you. The *you* that *is* Spirit will always make decisions that are best for all concerned.

Fasting As It Relates to This 40-day Practice

For millions around the world, fasting is the literal practice of not eating. Individuals will practice fasting for health reasons as much as for spiritual reasons and to ready oneself for enlightenment. With this 40-day Lenten Practice, the fast you are asked to do is to fast from all thoughts and speaking habits that break down your spirit and create an atmosphere of spiritual and mental toxic waste.

Should you choose to also *fast* from certain foods, or from additional habits, do this *mindfully* and not from a place of "should." One of the tenets supporting this Lenten Practice is non-suffering. Fasting should only be done if it supports another habit that you are already trying to secure in your life. The world has learned all it needs to from suffering. To take this idea even further, consider this: if any suffering is experienced during this practice, then it is likely that your focus is misdirected.

Setting the Stage for Transformation

This workbook has been created to support your spiritual liberation. We invite you to celebrate your innate wholeness and set your intention for this 40-day period. Perhaps your intention is simply to create the time to follow through on a daily practice—perhaps it is to deepen your consciousness, or perhaps it is to let go of fear or self-abuse. Or maybe there is something else that has called you to this book. Whatever brought you here, we want to assist you in creating your transformational experience.

Preparation

To make this 40-day period as powerful as it can be, prepare yourself. Take time to *mark your calendar* with the exact beginning and ending dates. If you chose to do this along with Lent, your dates will be already determined, although true Lent is longer than 40 days because Sundays are not counted. Be aware that the Lenten period always begins on Ash Wednesday and concludes on Easter, although the exact dates change yearly.

Set Your Intention

The best way to accomplish any goal is to be clear about your desired outcome. Take some time to think about what thinking habits you will be willing to surrender. Don't think too hard though—you will be given guidance throughout this workbook.

Take a few moments right now and get quiet. Invite Spirit to enter your awareness, and consider what it is that has called you to this practice. Take a minute and write out your intention.

My intention for this practice is to:

____

____

____

____

____

Support Your Success

To support your experience, consider doing this 40-day practice *with a partner.* Choose a prayer partner, a life partner, or a good friend. Whoever you choose to do this practice with, consider someone who has a high level of integrity and who will hold you accountable. This will surely improve your chances of success.

And lastly, *begin with the end in mind.* Beginning with the end in mind will help you in those moments when you find yourself struggling with this practice.

Reminders For Your Support

- Mark your calendar with a beginning and ending date.
- Set your intention; write it down.
- Consider working with a partner—remember where two or more are gathered, there is greater strength.
- Begin with the end in mind—stay clear about the purpose for investing this time.

How to Use the Exercises In This Workbook

Changing your mind is only part of your work. But keeping it changed is the challenge and the opportunity here. If you properly devote enough time, the next 40 days will be life transforming for you.

As you start your 40-day journey, remember to revisit the intention you have set for yourself often. If you have not already done so, go back to the previous page to the space provided, and write down your intention. Throughout the 40 days, you are given a variety of tools to use. Feel free to use them all. You will have the focus for the daily reflection with a journal exercise plus the "I am" statement that you can use throughout your day. There is also an additional Spiritual Practice to help you create the space for change in yourself.

Consider giving yourself the gift of allowing yourself time each day to read the daily message, incorporate the spiritual practice, and do the reflection exercise. Get by yourself for a few minutes each day, ideally in the morning or at the same time each day. While practicing at the same time each day is not essential, we believe it will help you to establish new habits that can fill the void that you are creating through releasing your old ways of thinking.

Begin each practice period by taking a moment to set aside all your worries for the time being and be present with the daily exercises. Know that anything you are concerned about can be addressed later. Relax the body and quietly invite the Great Universal Power to come into your mind and provide you with whatever information, memories, or ideas you need to fully utilize the daily practice.

Upon completing the practice, thank Spirit for its guidance and direction and invite It to be with you as you go through your day.

Enough said, let's get started!

DAY 1

Appreciation is a wonderful thing. It makes what is excellent in others belong to us as well.

—Francois Marie Arouet (Voltaire)

As you begin this journey, let us get started by letting go of our habitual practice of judging ourselves. We are usually our harshest critic. How many times have you heard yourself admonish yourself with statements like, "I'm so stupid," "I should know better," or "What's wrong with me?" When you catch yourself being too hard on yourself, ask yourself, "Is this really the truth about me?" and consider what you would say to someone else in the same situation. In most instances we would be much kinder to a friend or a colleague who found themselves in the same situation.

Today pay attention to the ways in which you judge yourself and be willing to release them. As you do the exercises for today, use them as a tool throughout the day to replace the negative judgments you hold about yourself.

Today's Spiritual Practice

Look into the mirror today and look deeply into your eyes and tell yourself how much you are loved.

DAY 1

Today I fast from thoughts of self-judgment.

Write a list of ten things—no less—that you love, honor, and respect about yourself.

I accept myself as I am and as I am not.

DAY 2

Forgiveness is choosing to love. It is the first skill of self-giving love.

—Gandhi

Forgiveness is the most effective Spiritual Practice that we have. It heals, reveals, and makes room for the new. A couple of key points regarding forgiveness that should be considered are as follows:

- It is never about condoning poor choices or behavior.
- It is not about letting anyone including you off the hook.
- If done proactively and on a regular basis, you will cease to create "new baggage."
- It is done so *you* can find true happiness again.

With this in mind, today we look at our birth family and the baggage we carry around about whom they are and the effect they've had on our life. Are there ideas or old wounds that no longer serve you? Whether our experience of our family is positive or negative, our judgments about them take up the space we could be using to simply accept them for who they are. It's from this place of acceptance that we begin to experience our family and the gifts we've received from them either directly or indirectly.

Today's Spiritual Practice

Pray in *your way* today for self-acceptance.

DAY 2

Today I fast from judging my family.

As I become mindful about how and what I judge my birth family for (even if I do not currently know them), I write a letter of gratitude for them, for their influence upon my life. This letter is a form of blessing that frees me from all negative energy and opens a space for freedom.

I am accepting my Divine Birthright of happiness.

DAY 3

Imagination gives man the ability to project himself through time and space and rise above all limitations.

—Charles Fillmore

Today ponder all the friends you have attracted and the gifts that they have brought you. Understand that some of these gifts are not as easy to recognize at first. Often times the very thing they have come to bring us is the thing that challenges us the most.

A very powerful question to ask oneself is this: Who will I be when this ______________ (fill in the blank) is healed? As you begin to imagine the shift, it will begin to take hold in your consciousness.

Today's Spiritual Practice

Get outside today for a minimum of ten minutes, breathing in fresh air, allowing it to clear away any clutter in your physical form.

DAY 3

Today I fast from judging my friends.

Make a list of your friends, the recognizable gifts that they have brought you, and ask yourself this: Through the healing of challenges with them, who have I become?

I am allowing grace to be fully revealed.

DAY 4

All that we are is the result of what we have thought. The mind is everything. What we think we become.

—Buddha

Watch your mind. During this time of fast, your mind will begin to judge you for your judging. Watch it, catch it, and forgive yourself for this habit. The key to success in this program is to be generously patient and loving with yourself. And forgive yourself very quickly.

Today's Spiritual Practice

Buy a one-stem flower and place it in a spot where you can see it all day or many times a day. Consider keeping a vase filled with your favorite flower all the time.

DAY 4

Today I fast from judging my judging.

Write a letter acknowledging your effort to renew your mind.

I am available to Spirit's full expression.

DAY 5

There was a time when a man was so convinced that the world was round that he was determined to prove it.

—Ernest Holmes

Someone once said that when they die, they want to leave this world being "all used up." To be all used up implies living life full out, paying "all" attention to what is possible and living into that possibility, and to express yourself fully each day.

So often we cultivate thoughts of limitations that are based on fear, failure, and humiliation, and considering we spend most of our time thinking, either we can think in affirming ways or in limiting ways.

Begin to spend your time affirming who you are, choosing to release negative thinking and deciding instead to choose thoughts that empower and expand your life.

Today's Spiritual Practice

Clean out a draw that is overflowing with junk. If something is usable and you're not using it, give it away.

DAY 5

Today I fast from thoughts of limitation.

Write a list of what you would do if you knew you couldn't fail. Allow yourself to dream and feel the dream as alive.

I am abundant in all ways.

DAY 6

The Universe must exist for the self-expression of God and the delight of God.

—Ernest Holmes

In order to live in a sustainable universe, it is our job to move away from competition and move toward cooperation. Cooperation implies that you feel safe and secure in this world. Anywhere that you see yourself in competition with anyone, affirm that there is always enough for all in this infinite universe.

Today's Spiritual Practice

Carry a notebook with you and record all good deeds that you witness and then share them with others.

DAY 6

Today I fast from thoughts of competition.

Begin to change your mind by writing down some new thoughts such as, "There is enough business for everyone," "There is enough love for all," etc. Stay at it until you complete ten new thoughts.

I am the expression of God's unlimited capacity.

DAY 7

To understand everything is to forgive everything.

—Buddha

Inherent within blame is shame. *But* when we learn to move away from blame and begin to practice responsibility, we begin to discover that we can set a new cause in motion. Shame separates you from the very thing that will support you in finding wholeness. When you replace blame with responsibility, you assume greater power, the kind of power that creates good in the world.

Today's Spiritual Practice

Sit in total silence today for ten minutes. No music, no phone, no book, no writing for ten minutes. Set a timer so you are undistracted and can be totally present.

DAY 7

Today I mindfully forgive myself for my mistakes.

Fast from self-blame; begin by making a list of all mistakes that you believe you've made. Begin your entry in this manner: I consciously and completely forgive myself for: (and make your list).

I am grace.

DAY 8

You will not be punished for your anger; you will be punished by your anger.

—Buddha

When practicing forgiveness, each time you are releasing anyone, remember to go into your heart and release them completely. Releasing the energy around someone is never the same as approving of their behavior; it is always about freeing your mind of any thoughts that hold you captive.

Today's Spiritual Practice

Spend no less than ten minutes blessing all of the world's religious and spiritual leaders.

DAY 8

Today I mindfully fast from blaming my priests/ministers/ spiritual advisors for any wrong guidance.

Become mindful of any spiritual or religious leaders that you hold any ill for, and write a statement of intention releasing them for any perceived wrongdoing.

I am open to God's grace.

DAY 9

To believe in a just law of cause and effect, carrying with it a punishment or a reward, is to believe in righteousness.

—Ernest Holmes

The next two days will compliment one another as you acknowledge your mother and your father. Be mindful that these 40 days are dedicated to developing a healing consciousness. Sometimes we have to touch an inner part of ourselves that is uncomfortable. You are here to be the one who guides healing. Mother is the single most emotionally charged role that exists. More people attach blame to mom than anyone else. Let's give her and this role a break. Be the one who begins to love objectively and do it *now*.

Her ignorance is not an excuse for anything that she might have done, but it will help you to open your heart for healing if you recognize that she simply was not skilled.

Today's Spiritual Practice

Light a safe enclosed candle today and keep it burning until it extinguishes itself. As you light it, acknowledge your ancestry.

DAY 10

Today I mindfully forgive my father for any real or perceived wrongdoing.

Today I write a letter blessing my father and releasing all stale energy and stories between us.

I celebrate my beauty and power.

DAY 11

It is the childlike mind that finds the kingdom.

—Charles Fillmore

Children are capable of such awful things. Although this happens out of pure ignorance and lack of experience, the things that children do leave their scars for a very long time. This is an opportunity to realize how bad things can happen from good people (children). This is your opportunity to be the mature one who wants to stand for love and stand for change. Simply declare that you are willing to forgive and move beyond your past; move beyond your history and watch as wonderful changes happen subtly inside of you. Even though these things happened a long time ago, anything that has left its mark on you must be released to be healed.

Today's Spiritual Practice

Carry a newspaper to one of your neighbor's door.

DAY 11

Today I mindfully forgive the peers of my youth for any real or perceived wrongdoing.

As you continue in this series of forgiveness, take time to recall old memories about your childhood friends and any pain that you have associated with them. Once again, record their names in your reflection practice with the intention of releasing them, one at a time. Do this mindfully and always with love.

I am walking in the love and light of all good all the time.

DAY 12

Teach and practice, practice and teach—that is all we have; that is all we are good for; that is all we ever ought to do.

—Ernest Holmes

According to Kahlil Gibran in the *Prophet*, your children are not your children. They are the sons and daughters of life longing for itself. You can have hopes and dreams and want for their success and health, but they will have their own ideas, ideals, and desires. Unless you free them to be who they are, you will be setting yourself up for a potential lifetime of pain and disappointment. Blame not, love, and accept more. If you are not a parent, consider freeing yourself from the expectations you accepted and integrated from your parents or family and allow yourself to be who you want to be.

Today's Spiritual Practice

Write a note to your grandmother/grandfather whether they are alive or not and thank them for their contribution to your life.

DAY 12

Today I fast from blaming my child/ren for not living up to my expectations.

Write a note to your child/ren and set your intention to accept them exactly as they are and free them from any expectations. Be generous in your offering. This will cause a magical albeit subliminal response blessing both you and your child/ren. If you are not a parent, forgive yourself for the kind of child *you were* letting go of any unmet expectations that were placed upon you.

I am the movement of Spirit.

DAY 13

I do not believe that God has imposed suffering upon anyone to punish them or to teach them a lesson.

—Ernest Holmes

One's job or career can be a real source of pain and disappointment. For many people, your place of employment can consume a lot time, energy and is a breeding ground for upset and disappointment. Your employers might already be delivering to you what they can. They might be at the end of their learning curve, or perhaps, your employer has reached its capacity. Acknowledging this will be helpful, but judging your employer for their limitations won't. Be generous and gentle for that energy always comes back to you from directions that you could never suspect. Forgiveness *never* means that you must stay in the status quo, but forgiveness will free the energy necessary to move on with greater ease.

Today's Spiritual Practice

Approach the next job or chore that you have to do but don't like to do (cleaning a toilet, for example) with great love and pride.

DAY 13

Today I mindfully forgive my boss/job/superiors.

Write a note acknowledging your employers for doing the best they can. Fast from the typical judgment and anger that comes with working. If you are self employed, write it to your most challenging customer. Don't send it to anyone; just write it for your own understanding.

I am compassionate with myself and others.

DAY 14

We can no more do without spirituality than we can do without food, water, shelter, or clothing.

—Ernest Holmes

God/Spirit/Life/Energy/Universal Love are all names for the same incredible, powerful, and creative energy of Life. This Essence does not form itself specifically as good or as something negative that is independent from the mold that you provide in the form of the thoughts that you think or the prayers that you pray. God did not place in your mind the thoughts that you think that guide your decisions neither does it place your prayers in your heart. It is the use of your free will that directed your thoughts and your prayers. God is that Essence and Power that simply says "Yes" to whatever it is you provide in the way of thoughts, prayers, or desires. That is to say, God is not responsible for what has happened in your life.

And lastly, God does not need *your* forgiveness. Forgiving God is the practice of freeing yourself from a sense of debt and blame.

Today's Spiritual Practice

Take time to notice the sky today, the clouds, the moon, or even the rain. Just notice it.

DAY 14

Today I mindfully forgive God/Spirit.

Sometimes we come through life without proper training in how to *do life powerfully.* We blame God for our lives not turning out the way that we had hoped it would. Take some time out today and take responsibility for your life and forgive God for what you think It was responsible for. You do this by simply declaring that you are responsible.

I am expressing my full potential.

DAY 15

In the pursuit of happiness, half the world is on the wrong scent. They think it consists in having and getting, and in being served by others. Happiness is really found in giving and in serving others.

—Henry Drummond

As much as one might be tired of hearing this, your best teachers are the ones living right under your roof with you. They are your intimate relationships, your immediate family, your spouse, and your children. It is through the individuals that you spend the most time with that you get to hone your human skills. As we grow and learn from these individuals, we get to see our "shadow" side. Our shadow is the part of us that lives within who we are; although we can recognize this part of our self, often we do not want to take ownership of this side of our personalities. As we learn to love the aspects of ourselves that get uncovered through others, we begin to embrace more of who we are and then begin to experience our wholeness. *It is imperative that through out this process, you follow these three tenets; Be gentle with yourself, be patient, and be compassionate.*

<u>Today's Spiritual Practice</u>

Spend time daily seeing yourself and your entire family as whole, perfect, and complete.

DAY 15

Today I am grateful for the good in my family.

Your family is a gift to you in more ways than you can imagine. Begin to take stock of your family, their gifts, their strengths, and what you have learned about yourself because they were in your life. In other words, who are you today because of them? (Focus on the positive)

I am accepting of my Divine birthright.

DAY 16

Begin to act from your dominion. Declare the truth by telling yourself that there is nothing to be afraid of, that you no longer entertain any images of fear.

—Ernest Holmes

Energy follows your attention. Now is the time to learn to capture your limiting thoughts and transform them into thoughts that redirect your attention to the positive. At first, this might take some work on your part, but after a short while—most likely by the end of this time of cleansing—you will begin to feel a sense of relief. The relief is because as thoughts of fear and worry weigh heavier on you, they take more of your energy, while positive faith-based thinking is lighter, easier and just leaves you feeling happier.

Fear is a collective disease, and it hides everywhere in your mind and actions. Stalk it out and declare its demise.

Today's Spiritual Practice

When you wake, set your intentions on having a good and glorious day.

DAY 16

Today I fast from all thoughts of fear and move into faith.

As you catch your fear-based thoughts and turn them into faith statements, write these down and then watch what the mind does. For example: “I don’t have enough money.” becomes “I will always have enough money for my needs.”

I am moving in the grace of Spirit.

DAY 17

It is impossible for a man to conceal himself. In every act, word or gesture he stands revealed as he is, and not as he would have himself appear to be. From the Universe, nothing is or can be hidden.

—Ernest Holmes

The moment you compare yourself to someone else, you are in denial of your good. The quicker you turn your attention away from comparison and turn it to acceptance, the quicker all of your attributes and qualities will come into the light. We live in a highly competitive society, and we have been bred over the years to *fight* to get on top when the truth is there is no real top. Would being on top mean being the one with more money or the one with more love or land or children? There is an infinite number of ways to discount our good. Let us begin to accept ourselves exactly as we are and feel blessed for our uniqueness.

Today's Spiritual Practice

Sit and imagine the entire world, happy, healthy, fed, and without borders.

DAY 17

Today I notice when I compare myself with others and turn to bless myself and the one I am comparing myself with.

Be fair and objective about who you are, your uniqueness, and your gifts. Throughout the day, wherever you catch yourself comparing yourself to anyone or any person, *stop* and bless that person. Take note today of the places where you seem to compare yourself and how you feel when you do this.

I am authentic in my expression.

DAY 18

All causes are essentially mental, and whosoever comes into daily contact with a high order of thinking must take on some of it.

—Charles Fillmore

"There is only *now*" is not a mere spiritual platitude. It is the truth. Now is the only time you have. Anything else is an illusion and yet most people spend most of their time pondering and pining over the past or waiting for some miraculous future to arrive. While you might be pondering or living in regret, you are losing your *now*. This precious moment in time is all you have; it is your job to suck the last bit of juice out of each moment. Even the practice of being present to anyone you are talking to, by looking directly into their eyes, will make the current moment more valuable. If you are struggling to stay current, it might be that you simply do not like your life. If this is so, then you will know that it is time to make a difference in your world.

Today's Spiritual Practice

Today spend a bit of time communing with nature. Go for a walk, hug a tree, count some stars.

DAY 18

Today I notice where my attention is and bring it back to the present and cease dwelling in the past.

You've heard the old adage: "Be here now." Today, practice staying present. Keep your attention on today, your now, and your here. At the end of your day, record in your reflection practice the places where you struggled most to stay present. What had the greatest pull? This can be very revealing.

I am experiencing my greatness today.

DAY 19

Words are also seeds, and when dropped into the invisible spiritual substance, they grow and bring forth after their kind.

—Charles Fillmore

Only individuals who think they do not have a life worthy of greatness have the time to gossip about others. Gossip is one of the most socially acceptable, powerfully destructive, and toxic habits that exist. Gossip is everywhere; it is how most of us communicate. Pay attention and notice what people are saying; once you begin to notice it, you will be shocked. Then you will see that most of the gossip is not even anchored in facts. Gossip is practiced by individuals that have nothing unique or important to say, so they turn to talk about others. Take yourself out of this category. Share your heart and soul in conversation; talk about your dreams and desires. Do anything other than talk about other people. Your friends and family will feel safer around you as they see you do this. Be a clear vessel for good by practicing non-gossip.

Today's Spiritual Practice

Be responsible for generously complimenting someone today. Watch as they feel appreciated.

DAY 19

Today I cease all gossip about others.

Pay attention to what catches your attention when you are tempted to gossip. Write about what you get from gossiping. How do you feel? Where do you get hooked? If you give up gossiping, consider what you will talk about?

I am the face of love.

DAY 20

You yourself, as much as anybody in the entire universe, deserve your love and affection.

—Buddha

Whether you are gossiping about yourself or someone else, the effect is equally damaging. Sometimes we forget who we truly are, and we act out of a low-level surface idea of who we think we are. If you knew who you truly were, what you are capable of expressing, you would live in *awe*. Lend yourself to this practice today. How you *choose* to see yourself is at the heart of who you are and how you are seen by others. Remember you are so much more than what you have thought of in the past.

Today's Spiritual Practice

Today anonymously leave a note of appreciation for someone who needs it.

DAY 20

Today I cease all gossip about myself.

Today, write a few paragraphs about how you want to be remembered when you are gone. What would you like others to *say* about the gifts you left behind on this planet? (Be creative and think *big*).

I am expressing my full potential.

DAY 21

If the only prayer you ever say in your entire life is thank you, it will be enough.

—Meister Eckhart

Did you have one of those mothers that always said, "If you don't have something nice to say, don't say anything at all." As youngsters, this piece of wisdom was lost on most of us, but it is one of the smartest things we were ever told to do. Even His Holiness the Dalai Lama charges us to gather the discipline necessary to resist ever saying a mean word. When your mouth and your words become an endless fount of love and beauty, the landscape of your world will reflect this practice.

Today's Spiritual Practice

Sit and listen to music while doing *nothing* else. Choose music that moves you.

DAY 21

Today I speak only compliments.

As you go about your day, compliment everyone, including yourself. If you have to, go through the effort and call people just to give them compliments. Catch your family, and especially your children, doing something right, and compliment them. Be generous; compliment everyone for the smallest possible things. Watch and see what happens.

I am the very essence of love.

DAY 22

God gives some more than others because some accept more than others.

—Ernest Holmes

Many years ago, before Oprah Winfrey brought to the public eye the practice of writing a *gratitude journal*, I had started a journal of the same nature out of my absolute need to change my mind and keep it changed. I was in a dark place and needed to pull myself back from the edge of what seemed like disaster. Somehow I knew intuitively that I needed to start changing what I looked at and focused on each and every day. Each night I began to write down something good about my day, my blessings, that which I normally took for granted. Sometimes I wrote the same things down over and over again. I know that I repeated things like this one: I am so thankful for the use of my hands, my feet, and my eyes. But I really meant it, and I began to find value where before I was taking things for granted. I would do this before going to bed, and I read it first thing every morning. This simple practice pulled my attention back to my good, and my world started transforming according to my shift in consciousness.

Today's Spiritual Practice

Write a letter of gratitude to yourself.

DAY 22

Today I find what is good in my world.

Begin to practice beauty by noticing what is good in your world. Before going to bed, read this list nightly. Make the list long and sincere and remember the good that you often take for granted, like your eyesight, this free country you live in, and the beating of your heart.

I am in the room [world] to heal the room [world].

DAY 23

Life is ever giving of itself. We must receive, utilize and extend the gift. Success and prosperity are spiritual attributes belonging to all people.

—Ernest Holmes

It is relatively easy to remember to thank someone for doing something nice or for doing something that you didn't expect. But if you really want to enjoy the energy that is generated through gratitude, begin thanking individuals for jobs that they are required to do. Go ahead, send out those note cards but also remember to thank people right in your own home. Thank your spouse, partner, lover for what they do every day—even if it is their responsibility. Thank your children for taking off their shoes or taking out the garbage—say thank you for anything. Let your home be filled with the vibration of appreciation. You can even leave notes taped on the door of your loved one or on their bed.

Today's Spiritual Practice

Go for a walk, bring a plastic bag with you, and pick up garbage that you didn't drop.

DAY 23

Today I thank people for everything they do and more.

Buy some note cards and send at least five handwritten notes of appreciation over the next week to anyone, for anything that you have noticed in your world. Be sincere and always be generous. Your generosity benefits you more than the one you are thanking.

I am walking in the light of God.

DAY 24

We are shaped by our thoughts; we become what we think. When the mind is pure, joy follows like a shadow that never leaves.

—Buddha

Gandhi said, "Be the change that you want to see in the world." These are some of the truest words ever spoken. Unless you are a very practiced or enlightened human, it is quite difficult initially to transcend what you see in the news and not be affected by it. To not be affected takes practice, a lot of practice. As you take on this spiritual practice of not watching or reading the news over the next ten days, remember *you* are the peace, *you* are the compassion, *you* are the unconditional acceptance, and as you take that on your life will begin to move in a whole new direction.

Today's Spiritual Practice
Pray every day for our political leadership to lead with honesty, integrity, and objectivity.

DAY 24

Today I meditate on peace as I fast from all news for at least ten days.

As you enter this ten-day period of fasting from news, use your reflection practice today to write a prayer for global peace. Then make a copy of it and put it around your home and tape it to your television as a reminder to not watch the news and to not give it any power. Remember no news on TV, radio, or online—just ten days, that's all. Pay attention to how you feel doing this.

I am worth being heard.

DAY 25

Prayer is the peace of our spirit, the stillness of our thoughts, the evenness of our recollection, the seat of meditation, the rest of our cares, and the calm of our tempest.

—Jeremy Taylor

We, the universal We, share aspects of ourselves that we wish were not part of us. But alas, they are, and the sooner we lovingly accept them and incorporate them into our spiritual practice, the sooner they will not have free expression. When we make room to love and accept ourselves from a place of *complete acceptance*, they have less power. Acceptance of our total "self"—all the parts—makes room for transformation. Take away the shame, and a new energy will emerge. This new energy will enlighten and empower you.

Today's Spiritual Practice

Write a note to your favorite grammar school teacher appreciating her/him—mail it or not.

DAY 25

Today I meditate on accepting myself exactly as I am.

Write a list in your reflection practice of all of the aspects of yourself that before now you have rejected. As you create your list, be gentle and loving. Begin each sentence in this manner: I now accept this aspect of myself which shows up as ____________ (controlling, self-absorbed, resistant, etc.), and I choose to love myself anyway.

I accept my Divine Nature.

DAY 26

To change and to change for the better are two different things.

—Old German Proverb

True liberation comes from awareness. Have you ever noticed that right after cleaning and dusting your home if you look back around you can see a bit of residual dust almost right away. Well, the judgments that are very destructive can make an appearance right after you do your mental housekeeping, which is why we must look and then look again. Whenever possible try not to judge yourself for your judgments; simply notice them and let them go.

Today's Spiritual Practice

Each time I find myself finding fault, I stop and take three breaths reminding myself that it is not necessary for me to form an opinion.

DAY 26

Today I release the more subtle judgments that seem to go unnoticed.

Today, ask yourself this: Where do I have quiet, righteous judgments about myself and others? Every time you notice them, write them in your reflection practice. Acknowledging when you are in judgment over time will support you in creating change.

I am functioning at my optimum.

DAY 27

The world is always ready to receive talent with open arms. Very often it does not know what to do with genius.

—Oliver Wendell Holmes

You are who you are for many reasons. Some reasons are because of choice and much is due to conditioning. Yet at your core is a place that resides that is the very essence of the vibration that birthed through you. Spirit (God) lives in all; it is your essence. And the sooner you turn to acknowledge how it shows up through your qualities, the sooner you get to feel more full and alive.

Today's Spiritual Practice

Begin to be extremely mindful when doing your chores.

DAY 27

Today I celebrate my true essence, which is pure.

Begin to take stock of your qualities. Begin to account for your good, the purity of your being. As you remember the moments of innocence in your life, record what you find. Try writing in different colors or with your non-dominant hand. See how you begin to wake up.

I am valuable in all ways.

DAY 28

We increase whatever we praise. The whole creation responds to praise, and is glad.

—Charles Fillmore

You are not a mistake; you are "on purpose." As you choose to believe this, you will uncover the place in you that remembers this. Our job is to remember who we are, to remember our good and our strength. There are many billions of people inhabiting this earth right now, and no two are alike. When you know this and can celebrate this with ease and grace, a sweet and natural confidence will begin to show itself.

Today's Spiritual Practice

Choose a spiritual book of any kind and read something each and every day.

DAY 28

Today I celebrate the self in me which is the Self of this beautiful Universe.

Write a paragraph about your connection to the universe. Where do you choose to see yourself in the greater scheme of things?

I am accepting myself as always worthy.

DAY 29

Three things cannot be long hidden: the sun, the moon and the truth.

—Buddha

This Lenten Practice, this cleansing, is about waking up to your good, but it demands your conscious participation. The Law of the Universe and the way that it functions is scientific and mechanical, but you are not. As a human, you are a fluid-free expression who gets to choose how you desire to be expressed. Once again, remember to be generous with yourself and begin by formulating a new direction of your thoughts, your language, and your acceptance of good.

Today's Spiritual Practice

Pay attention to everything that you put into your mouth. Chew slowly and for a very long time.

DAY 29

Today I consciously accept all my good.

Write a statement declaring your intention to remain open to all your good all of the time. Begin this statement in this manner: I (your name) now declare and open to . . . (Remember to stay focused on the positive.)

I am naturally prosperous.

DAY 30

Life is a mirror and will reflect back to the thinker what he thinks into it.

—Ernest Holmes

There is an Intelligence in this universe. We each identify with it in a different way. Some call it God, some call it love or energy or Spirit. No matter what name you use, it is available to you, and having a relationship with it on your terms is a way of inviting in a good friend for a safer and more intimate relationship. Feel free to express yourself as you feel moved to. You don't have to explain yourself to anyone.

Today's Spiritual Practice

Be in service to someone today. Offer someone a ride, a hand, or a cup of tea.

DAY 30

Today I thank Spirit for its place in my life.

Take some time today to contemplate Spirit's place in your life and then write a love letter to Spirit as you know that it resides within you.

I am the natural movement of Life expressing Itself.

DAY 31

Peace comes from within. Do not seek it without.

—Buddha

If speaking one prayer of affirmation changed our life totally and forever, the world would be completely different. Transformation takes dedicated time. Repeating this 40-day Lenten Practice yearly will continue to help you clean out the cobwebs that reside in your subconscious. Similar to a physical cleanse, it must be repeated, because just by proxy of living in the world, we are influenced subconsciously by everything around us. You don't just brush your teeth once and forget about it, do you? Well, you don't just cleanse your mind once either. The good news is that every time you do this, you dive deeper into faith, and the process gets easier and gentler on you. Be patient with yourself. You're doing the best you can.

Today's Spiritual Practice

Pray today in *your way* for a cause that really matters to you.

DAY 31

Today I begin again, watching my thoughts, fasting from fear, and diving into faith.

The more mindful we become of our thoughts, the clearer we become; however, there is always more work to do. Write out your intention to live from faith.

I am yes.

DAY 32

Thousands of candles can be lit from a single candle, and the life of the candle will not be shortened. Happiness never decreases by being shared.

—Buddha

Jealousy lives because we don't feel like we are enough, and it is never about the other person. It also exists because we believe in limitation as we think that there is only so much good or so much love or so much abundance. When we entertain feelings of jealousy, we are also suffering from a slow death of our true expression. This will take a bit of faith, but try it. Bless the person that you are jealous of. Bless the money someone has. Bless the home they live in. Do it with as much real feeling as you can muster and see how your focus brings you into a new experience.

Today's Spiritual Practice

As you are speaking to someone, look them straight in the eye. Not in a way that will intimidate them but in a way that they will feel seen.

DAY 32

Today I fast from jealousy and offer blessings instead.

Take some time to bless anyone whom you have thought yourself to be jealous of. Instead of restricting yourself that way, be a source of good, of support; be the one that stands in the light of love.

I am precious.

DAY 33

The talent of success is nothing more than doing what you can do well, and doing well whatever you do without thought of fame. If it comes at all it will come because it is deserved, not because it is sought after.

—Henry Wadsworth Longfellow

Success can look like many things. But in order to see it, you must begin to look for the small successes and give yourself credit. All of the great inventors, artists, and athletes are experts at failing. It is *through* their failing that they got to their success. Michael Jordan is famous for sharing how many times he failed at the foul shot before he achieved his level of greatness. Thomas Edison didn't fail in his 6,000 attempts to find a filament that would work to create the light bulb; rather, he succeeded in the 6,001st attempt. Success is an attitude—not a statement of fact.

Today's Spiritual Practice

Give away clothes that you no longer wear. Give them to an organization that will receive them with love.

DAY 33

Today I fast from thoughts of failing, and declare my success.

Take inventory of your large and small successes. Don't stop until the page is filled.

I am success in all ways.

DAY 34

Any fool can make things bigger, more complex, and more violent. It takes a touch of genius-and a lot of courage-to move in the opposite direction.

—Albert Einstein

Meister Eckhart said, “If the only prayer you ever say in your entire life is thank you, it will be enough.” No truer words have ever been spoken. Gratitude breeds a healthy prosperous attitude. As you begin to cease the habit of complaining, you will find more energy to be happy and fully expressed than you ever thought that you had. And while you are taking on this new habit remember to stop complaining about yourself as well. You are more abundant, more worthy, more gifted than you could possibly imagine. Zig Ziglar, a motivational speaker, once said, “If you don’t think that every day is a good day, try missing one of them.”

Today’s Spiritual Practice

Spend some time doing something creative and not familiar. Buy some new pencils, markers or pastels, and paper, and free your soul.

DAY 34

Today I fast from complaining and instead turn to gratitude.

As you begin to notice how much you might complain, place money in a jar for each time you hear yourself complaining. At the end of a month, donate this money to any source of your inspiration or to a cause that inspires you. And then do some research online to see how many individuals live at poverty level, or have *no* food, or no shelter. You will stop complaining quickly.

I am always provided for.

DAY 35

When prayer removes distrust and doubt and enters the field of mental certainty, it becomes faith; and the universe is built on faith.

—Ernest Holmes

Worry is a down payment for what you *don't* want. The focus of worry is the very same as speaking a prayer except that it is usually subtle, quiet, and filled with ill feelings that "sicken" the one worrying. Worry is one of the worst habits that exist. It never produces anything other than more upset. *But* if you notice that you are in worry and you remember to take what you are worrying about and formulate a new idea, a prayer so to speak, for this limitation, now you are choosing to be part of the solution. Take your worry and make it work for you and for the one that you are worrying about.

Today's Spiritual Practice

Pick up the newspaper and pray for the hardships and struggles that you read about.

DAY 35

Today I fast from worry and move to prayer for the opposite.

Worry is an investment in what you don't want. As you begin to recognize this, take your attention and write affirmations for how you really want to use your thinking time. For example, if you are worried about your children's health or college tuition, write an affirmation claiming perfect health for them or to acknowledge that their college is fully paid for.

I am healthy in all ways.

DAY 36

The universal Mind contains all knowledge. It is the potential ultimate of all things. To it, all things are possible.

—Ernest Holmes

In order to change the direction of your life, first you must *decide* what that new direction will be. It will take some amount of effort, but finding the silver lining is a habit that can be cultivated. Once you learn to look for that silver lining, you will find that it is more obvious and more available than you once thought. So put pen to paper and begin to declare and accept your good.

Your mind does not know the difference between a "felt" experience that actually happened and a "felt" experience that you imagined. It will respond with positive feelings equally. Declaring your good, writing it, and stating it, starts your mind in a new direction, and once you have redirected your attention, you will begin to find evidence very quickly to support the new and more empowering idea.

Today's Spiritual Practice

Meditate for ten minutes on the perfection of your heart.

DAY 36

Today I fast from feeling discouraged and turn to possibility.

We feel discouraged when we think we are at a dead end and have no options. But during this 40-day Lenten Practice, you are here to practice believing in possibility. A belief in possibility exists by choice. Take the things that henceforth you felt discouraged by, and write declarative statements of the possibility of them turning around, such as, if you felt discouraged about not paying your mortgage, your new declaration would be as follows: My mortgage is paid in full with ease and grace. Then act on this wisdom and do the next right thing.

I am power.

DAY 37

A state of expectancy is a great asset; a state of uncertainty-one moment thinking "perhaps" and the next moment thinking "I don't know"—will never get desired results.

—Ernest Holmes

It is easy to boost one's own self-esteem by finding what's wrong with others or by pointing out faults. However, this doesn't really boost your self-esteem at all. It actually restricts how you show up in the world because when we boost ourselves by looking at the negative, it does nothing for our true good. So many of the habits that we are looking at during this time of mind-cleansing, need our ceaseless and undivided attention. We must continue to remove them, similar to weeding a garden of those pesky weeds that keep sprouting up almost before our eyes. As we turn our attention from the habit of pettiness to thoughts of praise and generosity, our hearts will open and our attitude will produce happiness.

Today's Spiritual Practice

When you go to sleep tonight, go to sleep counting your blessings.

DAY 37

Today I fast from pettiness and turn to generosity.

Pettiness, like so many other things, is born of a consciousness that does not feel full. Take a look at the pettiness (which is usually about people) that might exist in your life and write affirmative, generous statements about these individuals—even if you don't believe it. *Find their good*. You can always find something good about a person.

I am the expansion of my consciousness.

DAY 38

Oh God, help me to believe the truth about myself, no matter how beautiful it is.

—Macrina Wiederkehr

Without guidance that is steeped in the belief in possibility, the influence that exists at a subliminal level is one of fear and caution. The fear of failure is huge, and often, the fear of success is even bigger. Don't let yourself deny your good and brilliance due to a little or a lot of fear. You've heard this quote: "Feel the fear and do it anyway." If you don't try, how will you know? And if it doesn't work out the first time, get up and try again. While you are doing all of this, *enjoy the ride, enjoy what you learn, and pat yourself on the back for the mere attempt.* Let yourself dream. Create that vision board that you have wanted to create. Join or create a mastermind group. Secure that business name that you have been dreaming about. Take a chance. Leap.

Today's Spiritual Practice

Give some money away today to a cause that you *do not* have anything invested in. Make it completely not about you.

DAY 38

Today I fast from saying "no" to good ideas out of fear, and begin saying "yes."

What are those wonderful, brilliant, and exciting ideas that you let go by because you were afraid. What would you do if you weren't afraid of failing? Begin to say *yes*, begin to think *yes*. If *yes* was your default, what inspirations would you follow through with and set free? Write them down.

I am embracing my intelligence.

DAY 39

You are important enough to ask and you are blessed enough to receive.

—Wayne Dyer

Similar to the belief of not being worthy, not believing that you are enough is the second significant foundational belief that undermines our good. Again, it is not true! You simply have not received the guidance and the support to teach you otherwise. You are enough, you were born enough, have always been enough, and will leave this earthly plane as having been enough. Your job is to remember it, recall it, and bask in the light of knowing this.

Today's Spiritual Practice

Cook something simple, set the table for yourself, and sit and dine in silence.

DAY 39

Today I fast from thoughts of I am not enough.

Throughout my day, I stalk any places in my mind where thoughts live, that support the old idea of *I am not enough.* As I catch them, each time I catch them, I declare my truth. The truth is I was born enough, I am enough, and I will always be enough. My *enough* is not determined by anything other than my Divine birth right and that birth right cannot be taken away or dulled by anything, any idea, or any person. I live into my *enoughness* every time I remember and practice this truth.

I am the natural movement of Life expressing Itself.

DAY 40

Worthiness or un-worthiness is something that is pronounced upon you by you. You are the only one who can deem yourself worthy or unworthy.

—Ester and Jerry Hicks

There is a truth, albeit unfortunate, that we as humans share. This truth is an underlying belief that we are not worthy. Of course, it is not Truth with a capital "T," but it is a truth as we have accepted its conditioning at the human level. It is one of the most fundamental and critical beliefs that we must learn to counteract. Even though this is a focus for this day, it would benefit you to remember this *always: I am worthy, worthy of my good, as it was birthed into my being.*

Today's Spiritual Practice

Write a love note to God.

DAY 40

Today I fast from thoughts of I am not worthy.

"I am not worthy" is a disease (dis-ease) in this society. It is shared by most of us, and it is one of the greatest lies that we perpetuate. Today, every hour on the hour, take time to stop and silently declare to yourself—*"I am worthy."* Write in your reflection practice about what you would do differently if you always remembered this Truth about yourself.

I am worthy of all good.

Well, congratulations, you have completed your 40 Days to Freedom Practice, and now it is time to really start practicing. "What? There's more?" you might say, but hear me out. 40 days is enough time to alter the course of your thinking, but just like exercising your body, you must maintain the mental and spiritual muscle you have created. As long as you walk this planet, you will continue to fall asleep and forget your true nature of wholeness. If you like what you've seen and want more of this, then you need to continue to wake up, take stock of your life, and work these principles that you have been working with these last 40 days.

In life, there is no *done*. You'll be done when you are dead and that will only be with this version of you. As long as there is breath in your body, there is intelligence. Where intelligence exists, the possibility of transformation exists. One thought at a time, one action at a time, *one day at a time*.

Don't fret if you did not complete the full 40 days. No worries. Just do it again and again until you have received all the good that this workbook has to offer, or go back and just complete the day or days that you missed. Hopefully, you have made the connection between your thinking and the conditions of your life and can see the value of this practice.

As you go forward, pay attention, watch your mind, and watch your habits, remembering to be patient and loving with yourself as you return to the Perfect Being that you are. Remember you were born perfect, and this perfection resides in you as the *Godspark* that is the truth of your being.

Have a good, glorious, and grace-filled life!

Other reading suggestions:

30-Day Mental Diet—Willis Kinnear
40 Day Mind Fast Soul Feast—Rev. Dr. Michael Beckwith
Radical Forgiveness—Colin Tipping
The Four Agreements—Don Miguel Luiz
The Dark Side of the Light Chasers—Debbie Ford
The Science of the Mind—Ernest Holmes

Edwards Brothers,Inc!
Thorofare, NJ 08086
19 January, 2011
BA2011019